Breath
of Wilderness

The Life of
Sigurd Olson

Kristin Eggerling

FULCRUM
GOLDEN, COLORADO

For my fellow adventurers and main men: my husband and life partner, Paul Blomquist, and sons Soren and Finn, and my dad, Don, who instilled in me his love of reading.

With gratitude to Robert K. Olson, Kevin Proescholdt, Candy Fleming, Dave Dempsey, Chuck Wick, and Alanna Dore of the Listening Point Foundation; David Backes, Jeannine Kellogg, Jim Moore, Susan Perry, Blake Hoena, Will Steger, Kate Thompson, Molly Beth Griffin, and Nicole Rom of the Will Steger Foundation; Karen Pick, Carolyn Sobczak, Melanie Roth, and others at Fulcrum Publishing; Karen Backlund, Bette McCormick, Darby Nelson, and Linda Middlestadt of the Great Lakes Visitor Center; the staff at the Minnesota History Center Library and the Ely-Winton Historical Society; the Northwest Minnesota Arts Council; the McKnight Foundation; and everyone else who provided assistance or advice. I am especially grateful for Sigurd Olson, who stood up for his beliefs in the face of tremendous adversity.

Text © 2014 Kristin Eggerling
Photographs courtesy of the Olson family: 1, 2, 3, 4, 5, 6, 7, 8, 10, 13, 14, 19, 20, 21, 24. Photographs courtesy of the Listening Point Foundation: 9, 11, 12, 17, 18, 22, 23, 26, 27, 28, 29, 30, 35, 38, 39, 40, 41, 43. Images courtesy of the Ely-Winton Historical Society: 15, 16, 25, 36, 37. Photographs by Kristin Eggerling: 33, 34, 42, 44. Images used with permission of the Minnesota Historical Society: 31, 32.

Library of Congress Cataloging-in-Publication Data

Eggerling, Kristin.
 Breath of wilderness : the life of Sigurd Olson / Kristin Eggerling.
  pages cm
 Summary: "Breath of Wilderness is the story of Sigurd Olson's love for wild places and how that love transformed his life. It inspired him to play a key role in the movement to preserve wilderness throughout North America, including the Boundary Waters Canoe Area Wilderness, the largest lakeland wilderness in the country. Olson's successful writing career, born from his devotion, spread his fervor worldwide. This is a story of one man finding his passion and standing up for what he believed even in the face of tremendous adversity. Olson knew immediately that once the wilderness was gone, it would be gone forever. There would be no getting it back."--Provided by publisher.
 Audience: Age 9 to 12.
 Includes bibliographical references and index.
 ISBN 978-1-938486-10-4 (alkaline paper) 1. Olson, Sigurd F., 1899-1982--Juvenile literature. 2. Naturalists--United States--Biography--Juvenile literature. 3. Conservationists--United States--Biography--Juvenile literature. 4. Nature conservation--United States--History--20th century--Juvenile literature. 5. Wilderness areas--United States--History--20th century--Juvenile literature. 6. Outdoor life--United States--History--20th century--Juvenile literature. 7. Boundary Waters Canoe Area (Minn.)--History--Juvenile literature. I. Title.
 QH31.O47E44 2013
 508.092--dc23
 [B]

                    2013032573

Printed in The United States
0 9 8 7 6 5 4 3 2 1

Design by Ken Lockwood

Fulcrum Publishing
4690 Table Mountain Dr., Ste. 100
Golden, CO 80403
800-992-2908 • 303-277-1623
www.fulcrumbooks.com

Contents

Foreword

I was really excited to meet Sig Olson when I was in my teens. He was the first real conservation hero I met in person; for me it was like meeting a famous actor or rock singer. He had been working to protect, preserve, and defend the Boundary Waters wilderness for decades; he was a gifted writer; he was a guide and adventurer. He inspired me to follow my dreams.

Sig was a mentor and teacher in a variety of ways. We both kept nature journals starting at a young age. I would get up in the middle of the night to watch the stars and to document meteor showers. I would spend time observing flowers at school and in my backyard. I would study them until I learned every little detail about them. It was these skills that later allowed me to survive in harsh conditions like those in the Arctic.

Sig inspired me to write. He told me that writing, like nature journaling, took persistence and dedication. Sig was stubborn, but his persistence and stubbornness paid off when it counted. Thanks to Sig's leadership, and that of so many others, we now have in northeastern Minnesota one of the greatest wildernesses, a place surrounded by lakes and pine trees, where loons, moose, and wolves roam, and where you can venture only by foot and canoe.

—Will Steger, polar explorer, educator, and president of the Will Steger Foundation

Foreword

My father, Sigurd Olson, was a trailblazer through history and life. Through the thickets and confusions of his youth and times, he cut a trail to the world of beauty, love, order, and meaning in nature. Like any boy, he loved being out in the woods, learning about wildlife, hunting a deer, being educated by the stern lessons of the northern seasons. But he did not

Robert Olson (or Bob) and his brother, Sigurd Olson Jr., spent much of their childhood outdoors. Here their father, Sigurd Olson, shows them how to fillet a fish.

wander. Like an Indian guide he followed deer trails or snapped off branches to mark the trail he was making.

Even as a child, he knew how wonderful it all was. As a man he put it into words like a map for others to follow. He called it wilderness, not as an unmapped jungle but as an Eden for our hearts and souls.

The beauty of this book is that Kristin Eggerling has brought his story to a new generation of would-be Sigurds, at that age when we make our greatest decisions. These are not decisions about what we should do with our lives, or about how to make a living, but about discovering, like Sigurd did, what it is that we love and forging a trail of it through the wilderness of our own life and times.

—Robert K. Olson, president emeritus,
Listening Point Foundation

One

Daniel Boone Days

Sigurd Olson loved the forests, lakes, streams, and wild creatures more than anything else in the world. Born in Chicago on April 4, 1899, to Lawrence J. and Ida May Cederholm Olson, Sigurd later said, "I should have been born in a log cabin."

Sigurd Ferdinand Olson in 1899

When Sigurd, or Sig, as most people called him, was five years old, his mother took him to Lincoln Park just north of downtown Chicago. As they walked through a grove of maple trees, he was struck by the blazing colors of the leaves, vivid with fall oranges, reds, and yellows. It was a memory that stayed with him throughout his life.

Around the age of six, Sig moved with his family to northern Wisconsin, where he spent his childhood and adolescence. The Olsons first lived in the community of Sister Bay on the Door County peninsula. Life there was full of adventure for a boy who loved the outdoors. Sig ran free exploring the woods, shore, swamps, and orchards. At night he listened to the foghorns moaning in the harbor. Later, the family moved to Prentice, a logging and farming town in the north-central part of Wisconsin, and then finally to Ashland, in the far northern part of the state along Lake Superior, where he attended high school and college.

When they were young boys in Sister Bay, Sig and his older brother, Ken, often walked to school together. As Sig shuffled down the path in the early morning, his black lunch pail swinging on his arm, he heard the meadowlarks singing from the fence posts and the trilling of the frogs in the swampy grass.

Forgetting about the time, he knelt to touch the wildflowers that covered the ground. He marveled at the delicate sky blue petals before pressing his nose into them to breathe in their subtle fragrance. He thought to himself, "I love the music of the frogs, the birds, and the smell of wildflowers."

Ida May and baby Sigurd, Sig's brother Kenneth, and his father, L.J. (or Lawrence), around 1889 or 1890

Sigurd with his younger brother, Leonard, and older brother, Kenneth, 1908. Unlike Sig, Kenneth and Leonard had little interest in the outdoors. However, Sig and Kenneth shared a love of writing and were close throughout their lives.

Just then his brother Ken reminded him to hurry up or they would be late for school. Sig ignored him and grinned broadly as he picked a few of the flowers to give to his teacher.

"These will make Mr. Yates as happy as they make me feel," he murmured. He didn't care that his thoughtfulness would encourage his classmates to call him "Teacher's Pet."

Even at school he spent more time yearning for the outdoors than studying spelling. Mr. Yates, a strict teacher, conducted regular spelling bees by lining up all the students in a row along a crack in the floor and giving them each a word to spell. When a child misspelled a word, a look of displeasure crossed Mr. Yates's stern face, followed by a whack across the student's hand with a ruler.

More than once, Sigurd spelled a word wrong because he was distracted, staring out the schoolroom window and daydreaming about afternoon fishing plans. Mr. Yates, with the threatening ruler in his hand, would point first at the dunce cap, then at the corner. Seething, Sig grabbed the cap, shoved it on his head, and trudged over to the corner to sulk. "I wish I was outside," he grumbled to himself. Still, even though he struggled with spelling, Sig was drawn to words, feeling their beauty and poetry.

No one in Sig's family understood his love for nature, except for his grandmother, who lived with them. Sig and Grandmother shared a special bond because of their passion for the outdoors. She often waited for Sig to return from fishing to admire the trout he caught. Grandmother listened intently to his stories while frying the catch. Then they would sit together at the kitchen

Sigurd was especially close to his grandmother Anna Cederholm. Taken in 1916 in Ashland, Wisconsin, this is the last picture of her.

Sigurd and his trout. One of the first stories he wrote was "Grandmother's Trout," which he later included in his book *The Singing Wilderness*.

table and eat the feast with freshly baked bread and glasses of cold milk.

During these years, a time in his life he called his Daniel Boone Days, Sig liked to pretend he was Davy Crockett or Daniel Boone and escape by himself to the woods near his home in Prentice. It felt like stepping into another world. There he would create a bed of balsam branches to lie in and watch the birds above and the creatures around him. He found the wilderness mysterious and exciting, and he couldn't stand to be away from it for long. He later explained that he felt "at one with the great trees, with the birds and squirrels and trout and the sound of the wind in the branches."

One day, twelve-year-old Sig ventured into the woods, sat down on a log, and watched as a big doe appeared out of the shadows to drink from the bubbly creek for several minutes before leaping back into the darkness of the forest. As if a spell had been broken, Sigurd's stomach growled. Wanting to be a true wilderness man and live off the land, he hadn't brought along any food. He began to search for something to eat. Leaning over, he peered into a shallow spot of water next to the creek and discovered some clams. "Clams are supposed to be good to eat," he recalled, so he reached in and dug them out, gathered some sticks, and built a fire. He placed the clams on top, roasted them over the coals, and inhaled the smoky aroma. Once they were cooked, he used the shells for plates. Hot juice ran down his chin as he devoured his meal. His heart filled with admiration and love for the nature that surrounded him. He ate until his belly was full, then curled up on his bed of fragrant balsams. "I am as secure as a bear in a cave," he thought as he fell asleep, perfectly content.

Sig fished for trout or bass most days and hunted or trapped every chance he got. He especially enjoyed hunting for mallards or rabbits. Later, he skinned, prepared, and cooked the animals before eating them. Each step provided a greater connection with wildlife and was part of the adventure. One day the school janitor, Mr. Johnson, invited Sig to join him and his beagle hound to go rabbit hunting. Sig's excitement grew each time he saw a rabbit jump up in the alder thicket. The beagle sang as he chased the rabbits round and round before the boom of the shotgun rang out.

One afternoon, Sig grabbed a bucket and set off to pick cranberries. When he found the tart, red fruit hidden among the greenery, he filled the bucket to the brim and then started for home, eating a few along the way. As he wandered, a stirring caught his attention, and he turned to see what was making the noise. He couldn't believe it. Right in front of him was a bear. He tore off running faster than ever, tripped, and fell, dumping his berries into the bushes. Scared for his life, he shot up and bolted home. Even though the bear had frightened him, Sig couldn't stay away from the wilderness for long.

Young Sig was especially fascinated with squirrels and longed to have one as a pet. He thought that if he caught one he would be capturing a part of nature, making his life complete. Sig sat for hours and watched them gather nuts and chase up and down the trees, chattering constantly. He learned from an older boy how to construct a box trap and set to work to build one. He planned to catch a pair of squirrels and keep them inside the screen porch of his house.

One day he placed the trap on the end of a log and filled it with a handful of hazelnuts he had gathered. He lurked at the base of a great pine tree, noticing the brown and green needles that covered the forest floor. He listened to his heart pounding as he held his breath. Wishing he could become invisible, he imagined that he was a hunter waiting for his prey. He spied a squirrel peering into the trap. Then, in a flash, it scurried in and the trap door crashed down with a bang. He rushed over to make sure the latch was tightly shut, hastily grabbed the trap with the squirrel inside, and ran for home lickety-split. A few days later he returned and repeated the process, capturing its mate.

Sig cared for his pair of squirrels with complete dedication. He fed them the finest nuts and pinecones and lined their cage with the greenest, softest hemlock branches he could find. He unraveled an old sweater to make a comfortable nest. The squirrels adjusted to their new home and began to wait patiently for their meals. Sig grew mesmerized by their antics and loved studying the white rings around their eyes, the black stripes down their sides, and especially their bushy tails.

In the spring he noticed that the female had begun to line the nest with her fur, a telltale sign that she would soon have babies. Sig hovered around the cage like an anxious parent. One day he peered into the nest and found three soft, pink baby squirrels snuggled there. He was so excited, he couldn't eat or play and spent every moment he could near the cage. Later Sig reached down and picked up the babies one by one. He gently stroked their fur and fed them out of his hand. It was a dream come true for him, but it would be short lived.

The next day he returned home to discover the squirrels missing and a neatly gnawed hole in the screen. Frantic, Sig scoured the forest nearby and the woodpiles in his yard, but there was no sign of his beloved squirrels. He was grief stricken by what he felt was the desertion of his companions. His mother sat down with him and explained that squirrels are not pets. "They are wild creatures and belong in the wilderness," she told him. Sig still missed them, but he realized that she was right. The squirrels were better off in the wild.

Sig spent hours lying on the ground, listening to the sounds of the earth. He could hear the rustling of fall leaves and pine needles, but also the *chick-a-dee-dee* of chickadees, the *conk-la-ree!* of red-winged blackbirds, the hoot of an owl, and the wild, alarming scream of an osprey hunting for its dinner. The soaring birds made Sig jealous. "I wish I could fly and play hide-and-seek with the clouds," he thought. Frogs croaked and insects buzzed from a nearby pond. Suddenly, the honking of geese crowded out the other noises. "Where are they going and why?" he wondered as they flew by. And then he realized that he might not be the only one who was curious. "Boys all over the world could be seeing the same thing right now and wondering the same thing," he thought.

The little pond was also home to ducks, minks, and weasels. A muskrat house, built out of sticks, sat just above the water to keep the nest dry. Sig marveled at the animals and the green scum that produced bubbles on the pond's surface. As he watched all these forms of life interacting and coexisting, the realization hit Sig that all life is connected.

At the local library, Sig read about famous painters and admired their art. One day he bought some tubes of paint, a paintbrush, a palette, and a canvas. He grasped the brush, dipped it in the paint, and applied the colors to create the master-piece he saw in his mind, but it looked nothing like he had envisioned. The images were crude and

Sigurd's family home in Ashland, on the corner of Second Avenue and Sixth Street

unrecognizable. How frustrating! He kept trying, but the painting only looked worse. No matter how hard he tried, he was unable to express what he was feeling. Then he thought perhaps he could paint pictures with words instead.

Like other kids, Sig didn't always listen to his parents. When he was a young teenager, he and some friends saw men smoking in front of a nearby saloon. Sig's father, L.J., a strict Baptist minister, always told him that "smoking was a great sin," but Sig wanted to try it. He didn't have any tobacco or money to buy a pipe, but he'd heard that pipes could be made from corncobs and filled with dried bark and leaves, what some American Indians called kinnikinnick. He and some friends gathered corncobs and bark from a red willow tree and created their pipes. Later, the boys crawled under a big box, lit their pipes, and inhaled the bitter smoke. When they heard L.J. walking toward them, they rushed to extinguish and hide the pipes and began singing gospel songs they had learned in Sunday school. Sig's father peeked underneath the box and smiled as the boys sang louder. L.J. went into the house and told Sig's mom that the boys were so good, he expected they would become elders in the church.

Two

Decisions, Decisions

After high school, Sig attended Northland College in Ashland for two years. He wasn't sure what career he wanted to pursue, but he discovered that he enjoyed playing football and in no time became a talented athlete on the football team. One late October day, the sky was dark, and he sensed a storm brewing. He knew these weather conditions were perfect for forcing flocks of bluebills to take shelter in a nearby swamp. His heart began to beat faster in anticipation. Unfortunately, one of the biggest football games of the season, against Superior State College, was also that day. "What am I going to do?" he worried. "I can't let down my team." He heard the sound of the bluebills in his mind and imagined them riding the wind. He could almost see the flocks sailing in from the north out of the clouds.

Although he knew that he'd be in big trouble with his coach and the team, he couldn't bear to miss the birds. He quickly grabbed some gear and headed for the woods. When he returned to school on Monday, he learned that his team had lost the game. He felt like a criminal when his teammates glared at him. The coach kicked him off the team, even though he was one of the best players. "You should never play football again," the coach told him, ending his football career. While Sig felt shame, he knew in his heart that following the birds had been the right decision for him.

During Sig's first year of college, his friend Andrew Uhrenholdt invited him to the hospital to visit his sister, Elizabeth, who was recovering from pneumonia. When Sig stepped in the hospital room, he felt awkward and couldn't say a thing. He grabbed a pillow and threw it at Elizabeth before leaving. She was not impressed. Later, Andrew invited Sig to come home with him to his family farm near Seeley, Wisconsin, over the Easter holiday. Sig hit it off with Andrew's father, Soren, who suggested that Sig live and work at the farm that summer. Sig quickly agreed.

Sig flourished on the farm. He thoroughly enjoyed his time outdoors working on the land. Soren was easy to talk with, and Sig admired his strong conservation values. Sig also made a better impression with Elizabeth. The next fall Sig traveled to the farm regularly to work and to see Elizabeth.

Back at Northland College, Sig considered becoming a missionary. He knew this would please his father immensely. In L.J. Olson's eyes, there were

Elizabeth Uhrenholdt learned to love the outdoors as much as Sig did.

only three worthwhile professions: the ministry, farming, and teaching. After agonizing over the decision, Sig realized his heart wasn't in the ministry. He contemplated farming but decided that didn't feel right either. After he finished his second year at Northland, Sig attended the University of Wisconsin in Madison to earn a degree in agriculture and biology.

Sigurd with his bags packed, about to head to the University of Wisconsin in Madison

After graduation, Sig decided to try the only other option his father would accept: teaching. He moved to Nashwauk, a small town on the Mesabi Iron Range in northeast Minnesota, to teach high school. At the end of each school week, he packed some supplies and headed out camping for the weekend.

In the spring of 1921, Sig received an offer from a gold prospector to travel to Flin Flon in the far north of Manitoba, Canada, to pan for gold. He ached to go, but Elizabeth had had enough. She calmly and firmly told him that if he took the trip, she would not wait for him. It was the wilderness, or her. Sig would have loved the adventure, but he loved Elizabeth more, and the couple set a wedding date for that August.

Sigurd loved to fish and would have spent all of his time outdoors if he could have.

Three

The Meaning
of the Outdoors

In June 1921, another wilderness opportunity arose, and this one Sig couldn't pass up. With Elizabeth's support, Sig set out with two friends on a month-long trek east of Rainy Lake and north of the rugged shores of Lake Superior. It was during this canoe trip to the Superior Roadless Area along the Canadian border that the real meaning of the wilderness became clear to Sig.

Sig and his friends stood on the shores of Fall Lake, ready to head north, all the excitement of the adventure before them. They could hardly wait to explore the wild, unspoiled lake country and its thousands of miles of canoe routes. As Sig described the journey later, "And so we traveled through hundreds of lakes and rivers, drunk in the beauties of countless waterfalls, rapids and virgin forests." He had never encountered a world so remote and untouched and yet so full of life. One night after they'd finished a long portage, he sat under the spruce and Norway pine trees next to the lake. He was bewitched by the clear water, smooth as glass, and the glow of the sun reflected there. Rocky islands floated in the distance; loons laughed their wild, screaming call; the smell of balsam filled the air. "Everything is so exquisitely beautiful that I cannot help wonder if this is not a fairyland," he mused. He was enchanted by the splendor that surrounded him, a feeling that would change the course of his life forever. "I have fallen in love with a beautiful wilderness of lakes and rivers and forests known as the Quetico-Superior Country. I discovered … an emotional and spiritual significance that was not with me before."

Sig found complete happiness in the wilderness. He once said, "I am in love with the out of doors and all of its beauties, its waters, lakes, and trees and everything about it."

Shortly after Sig returned from that fateful trip, his brother Kenneth, editor of the *Milwaukee Journal,* asked him to write an article about his canoe adventure to the wilderness near Ely. Sig's account of the country that had taken hold of his heart poured out of him. The article, which also appeared in the *Nashwauk Herald,* was his first published article and marked the beginning of his long writing career.

On August 8, 1921, Sig Olson married Elizabeth Uhrenholdt under a white pine at her parents' farm. Sig said that he "was only half alive" when he was away from Elizabeth, and she felt the same. Elizabeth knew that Sig's need to spend time outdoors would be a fundamental part of their life together.

The day of the wedding, the couple broke the news to Elizabeth's parents that they would be heading into the wilderness for a three-week honeymoon. It would be Elizabeth's first canoe trip, and they'd be

Sig and Elizabeth celebrated their wedding outdoors with family and friends. Sig's father officiated the ceremony.

following a route neither of them had ever traveled. Worried about the couple's safety, Elizabeth's parents tried in vain to convince them to go to a resort or another more typical honeymoon destination. But Sig and Elizabeth had made up their minds. They took the train to Duluth and transferred to the Duluth, Missabe, and Iron Range Railway, rode one hundred miles farther to Ely, and continued to Winton, Minnesota, where they began canoeing at Fall Lake. They paddled and portaged over rivers and lakes, including Knife, Ottertrack, Saganaga, Kawnipi, Agnes, and Basswood, and saw only two other people the entire time.

When they returned that September, Elizabeth joined Sig in Nashwauk for a year. The next September, Sig enrolled at the University of Wisconsin in Madison to pursue an advanced degree in geology, but he stayed for just one semester. He felt

Elizabeth had never taken a canoe trip, but she quickly agreed when Sigurd suggested they spend their honeymoon canoeing in the remote wilderness.

homesick and restless and couldn't wait to get back to Elizabeth and the wilderness. Just then a job teaching biology opened at the high school in Ely, and Sig and Elizabeth jumped at the opportunity to move closer to the wilderness canoe country. Sig took his students outside as often as he could.

Sigurd liked to teach his biology classes outside. His passion for the wilderness and the land made a lifelong impact on his students.

Sig and Elizabeth embraced the Ely community and volunteered with many organizations. Sig became a scoutmaster with the Boy Scouts and led the boys on many wilderness canoe trips. At the end of the school year, Sig accepted a job as a wilderness canoe guide, a job he would continue to do for many summers that followed. After a few years he split his teaching time between the local high school and Ely Junior College, which later became Vermilion Community College.

Sig guided many camping trips for pleasure and as a paid guide. He is seen here on the far left with some unidentified companions.

The love and fascination Sig had for animals when he was a young boy never diminished. He had always wanted to ride a moose, and once he took the chance while canoeing with a friend. As they paddled next to one, Sig grabbed on to it, hoisting himself onto its back. He held on for dear life as the moose charged toward the shore. Sig planned to jump off the moose before reaching the shore, but he didn't let go in time, and he fell off as the moose ran up the riverbank. The moose, clearly unhappy about the uninvited passenger on his back, reared backward and landed on top of Sig, writhing and thrashing about. Fortunately, Sig escaped serious injury, suffering only sore muscles. It was a frightening experience, but he laughed about it later. Offering some advice about what he'd learned, he warned, "Never trust a moose no matter where you find one," and if you do, never get too close to shore without jumping off.

Although Sig was often busy sharing his love of the outdoors with others, he always found time to be alone in the wilderness as well. During one camping trip, Sig climbed Robinson Peak in Canada's Quetico Provincial Park. He observed the blue lake below and saw the smoke from his own campfire. As he looked out at the stunning wilderness landscape, the fiery sun dropped and began to disappear. He sat in the fading glow until there was only darkness, feeling an intense connection to the universe that stayed with him long after.

Sig on a canoe trip to Quetico Provincial Park in Ontario, Canada. He guided many canoe parties through un-mapped and unknown areas of the Quetico.

Sig and Elizabeth had two sons: Sigurd Jr. (or Junior), born in 1923, and Robert (or Bob), born two years later. Sig said he almost missed Junior's birth because it came on the opening day of duck hunting season. Both boys developed a strong connection with the outdoors. Years later Junior said, "I inherited a love of ... wild country and natural things ... [a] feeling for wild places."

Sigurd holding his first born,
Sigurd Thorne Olson, in 1923

Junior and Bob grew up in the wilderness, and theirs was a "Huck Finn" childhood full of adventure. When they were young, Sig often entertained them before bed with silly stories about the wild adventures of a moose with rubber horns and chipmunks named Roscoe and Boscoe. All year round, the Olson family spent their free time exploring the wilderness. Summers included canoeing, campfires, picnics, berry picking,

hiking, and fishing. The family took many camping trips, singing around campfires under clear skies. When fall arrived, the focus turned to hunting. One day while they were sitting in a duck blind together, Sig confided in Bob, "I never feel I am wasting my time when I am out of doors." Winter meant cross-country skiing, snowshoeing, ice fishing, and skating. Sometimes the family even skied before breakfast.

Sig instilled his love for the outdoors in both his boys, but his talk of almost nothing besides the wilderness wasn't always welcomed. At times his

Sig Jr., Elizabeth, Bob, and Sig snowshoed and skied in the early morning, after school, and under the stars during the winter nights.

passion overwhelmed and alienated his family and co-workers. "All we ever hear about is wilderness," Bob once said. The boys didn't understand why Sigurd, or Papa, as they called him, felt compelled to talk about it all the time. "He never thought about anything else," Bob reflected years later.

As a child, Sig had been fascinated by the French voyageurs who traveled Canada from 1650 to 1850 by canoe to trade fur and goods with the native peoples. He shared their love for the wilderness and found the stories of their romantic explorations full of adventure and intrigue. Now Sig hoped his boys would become modern voyageurs. On one canoe trip to Curtain Falls, the outlet for Crooked Lake, Sig told the boys stories of the wilderness men of Hudson's Bay who traveled down the chain of border lakes on their way to the Grand Portage Post at Lake Superior. To help the boys feel like they were part of the ancient tradition, he taught them the old French songs, and they camped and backpacked on the same trails the voyageurs used. The falls roared in the background as they landed at a smooth, black rock and got out of their canoes. Sig imagined that the boys were seeing the voyageurs' canoes landing at the same spot.

Sig himself joined a group of Canadian friends for yearly canoe trips that lasted about three weeks and covered approximately five hundred miles. The men paddled the routes of the voyageurs through Canada's Northwest Territories and Quetico-Superior Country. To invoke the spirit of the voyageurs, the canoeists read the original voyageurs' journals and sang songs as they followed in their footsteps. Sig's companions referred

Sigurd, nicknamed the Bourgeois, traveled Canada's waterways many times with a banker, an ambassador, a military major general, and a journalist. On those trips he dressed as a French voyageur, or fur trader, from years past. His outfit included a multicolored sash worn around the waist to strengthen the abdomen, moccasins, a buckskin shirt, and leggings.

to him as the Bourgeois, which is what the original voyageurs called their trusted leaders who were responsible for all major decisions. They relied on him to guide them and they gave him their total respect. Later fans of Sig's also called him Bourgeois.

Sig described love for the wilderness as a love for a way of life, a love of danger, comradeship, hardship, and challenge, and a love for all of its elements, including flowers, trees, rocks, sunsets, all creatures, wind, lakes, rivers, and solitude. In nature he always found a strong connection to the past. When he looked at a boulder, he pondered its history. What people had walked or sat here? What rains or snows had fallen on it? He thought about the glacial ice sheets and the people who had lived and hunted near them. What clothing had they worn? In his mind he could see the smoke from their fires and smell the sizzling meat in the air.

Sig showed Sig Jr. how to warm his hands over the fire. More than fifty years later, sitting in front of another fire, Sig Jr. remarked to his dad, "I've often wondered how many campfires we have sat around together."

Campfires were especially meaningful to Sig. He believed that each new campfire rekindled or brought back some experience from the past and that those who share campfires enjoy a special kind of comradeship. "My whole life has been a series of campfires," he said. When Sig gazed into the fire, he imagined past generations staring into campfires just as he was, dreaming of their own passions, hopes, and fears.

The wilderness had a powerful effect on Sig. Spending time there helped him to feel peaceful inside and taught him lessons about the world and about himself. He came to believe that there is nothing more important than protecting our wild areas, saying, "In saving any wilderness area, you are saving more than rocks and trees and mountains and lakes and rivers. What you are really saving is the human spirit. What you are really saving is the human soul."

Four
National Wilderness Scene

During the early 1920s, at the beginning of Sig's career as a teacher and wilderness guide, a threat to the canoe country wilderness transformed him into a conservationist. It shocked and angered Sig to learn that local chambers of commerce and the US Forest Service were proposing that a road be built to every lake in the Superior National Forest – what they called the "playground of a nation." The Forest Service wanted roads to allow them to fight fires more efficiently. The chambers of commerce wanted the roads for tourism. Sig realized that he had to act, but he wasn't sure how. Until now, he had taken it for granted that the land would always be there in its pristine, wild condition. But if roads were constructed to reach every lake, the wilderness near Ely would be destroyed. And he knew that once the wilderness was gone, it would be gone forever. There would be no getting it back.

As a wilderness guide, he had met and become friends with many national environmental leaders,

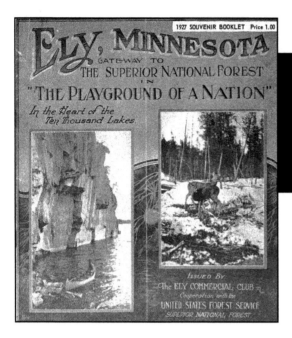

This brochure, published by commercial interests and the US Forest Service, promoted the construction of roads through the wilderness.

such as Will Dilg, the organizer of the Izaak Walton League, and Charlie Heddon, a famous fisherman and fishing tackle manufacturer. Sig also knew editors and writers for national publications, like Don Hough of the *Saturday Evening Post*, who shared his love for the wilderness near Ely. They too were alarmed when he filled them in on the plans to develop the region, and they promised to use their influence and knowledge to help protect the area by bringing national attention to the fight. Under their guidance, Sig wrote letters and attended meetings, eloquently expressing his convictions and applying pressure on the decision-makers to enact policies that would protect his beloved wilderness.

Sigurd's hard work paid off when a compromise was reached. The construction of two roads was allowed in the roadless Superior National Forest: the Fernberg Road east of Ely and the Upper Gunflint Trail. Later another road, the Echo Trail, was allowed. This was far less than what the Forest Service and the chambers of commerce had advocated for but still an unwelcome development for the conservationists.

Then in 1926, US secretary of agriculture William Jardine designated 640,000 acres of the national forest to be protected as wilderness, which would later become a significant portion of the Boundary Waters Canoe Area (BWCA).

Sig learned a great deal from that first battle, and those early efforts laid the groundwork for his future fights to save the wilderness.

That initial threat led to another. Also in 1926, lumber baron Edward Backus proposed the construction of dams at Kettle Falls, Curtain Falls, Upper Basswood Falls, and Saganaga and Knife Lakes to produce power along miles of shoreline in the area that at the time was called the Superior Roadless Area. This plan would have flooded hundreds of islands and several thousand miles of shoreland, obliterating the wilderness. One evening,

Sigurd paddled his canoe into the wilderness and imagined what the area would look like if the dams were built. "The mists might rise again," he wrote, "but the music of [this] hallowed place would be stilled forever, the enchantment gone. ... The islands lay like black silhouettes against the glow of sunset, the dusk [is] alive with the calling of the loons. ... It [seems] incredible that anyone would want to transform such a scene into kilowatts and profit, and I [know] in my heart nothing [is] more important than saving it. Man [needs] beauty more than power, solitude more than dividends."

Sig referred to himself as a "canoe man trying to get the rest of the world excited about saving ... the finest recreational resource on the continent, our wilderness canoe country."

And so Sigurd, along with other conservationists such as Ernest Oberholtzer, took on the developers. Once again, Sig shared his love, enthusiasm, and knowledge by writing and speaking to groups, individuals, and people in power.

While Sig was speaking up to protect the wilderness, he continued to help people experience it in person. In 1929, Sig and two partners, Wallie Hansen and Pete Peterson, started Border Lakes Outfitting Company. They provided equipment and guides for canoeists heading into the wilderness.

Sig became an owner/manager of Border Lakes Outfitting Company with two partners, Walter "Wallie" Hansen and Mervin "Pete" Peterson. In this picture he is standing in front of the outfitting company with Wallie Hansen.

Sig began to see results from his work to protect the wilderness when, in 1930, Congress passed the Shipstead-Newton-Nolan Act, protecting the shorelines of lakes and streams on federal land within the Superior National Forest. This did not prevent logging away from shorelines, though.

In the fall of 1931, Sig attended the University of Illinois in Champaign for one year, studying wolves and their predatory habits to earn a master's degree in animal and plant ecology. He was the first to study wolves, and his research proved to be a milestone in understanding the species, both for the scientific community and for himself. Before his close study of wolves, he had seen them only as killers and predators of deer. Afterward, he was a strong advocate for their protection.

He once wrote to a friend about a timber wolf that had crossed a trail where Sig stood: "It stopped beside a great boulder then turned to watch me not fifty feet away. It had a gorgeous black ruff over the shoulders and I could see the eyes. For a few moments we talked wolf-talk. ... Then it wheeled in the deep snow and plunged out of sight."

Sig loved learning, but school was not for him. Once again, he felt antsy in the classroom and couldn't wait to get back to northern Minnesota.

When he returned home, he continued guiding and managing his outfitting company in the summer and during the school year taught almost exclusively at Ely Junior College.

In 1933, the Minnesota legislature passed a law protecting state-owned shorelines within the Superior National Forest. The next year, the International Joint Commission of Canada and the United States, an organization that works to resolve disputes over waters on the borders of the two countries, recommended the denial of the proposed power plant plan. It had taken nine long years to ban the development, but thanks to Sig's persistence, the land he loved would be protected — at least temporarily.

Shortly after the power plant project was defeated, Sigurd began another fight: banning airplanes from flying over the Superior Roadless Area. In 1941, pilots began flying fishermen into the region from all over the United States. The number of flights escalated as pilots returned home after World War II. This flood of people led to resorts being built throughout the roadless area. The silence of the wilderness was overcome by the sound of airplane engines as planes flew over and landed nearby. On one canoe trip in

Knife Lake, Sig counted a plane every eight minutes for six straight hours.

On another trip, Sigurd and a companion paddled their canoe through a pale green mist. They observed a black bear scooping luminous fish out of a pool of water, while partridges drummed a low-pitched thumping beat in the distance. The air, rich with the smell of thawing humus, felt calm and peaceful. Trout splashed in the stream. Gradually, a dull drone grew louder and louder, and then they saw lights coming toward them. The pilot gunned his motor and landed his floatplane in the water nearby. Passengers disbanded, and the plane rose back into the sky as if it had never been there. Suddenly the trout were still,

Sig liked to quote his friend William O. Douglas, a US Supreme Court justice, who said, "We establish sanctuaries for ducks and deer and other animals. Is it not time that we establish a few sanctuaries for men?"

the loons were gone, and the tranquility of the wilderness had evaporated.

In 1948, Congress passed the Thye-Blatnik Act, which directed the secretary of agriculture to acquire resorts, cabins, and private lands within two-thirds of the future BWCA. This helped eliminate many of the privately owned resorts and cabins in the wilderness and was a step toward banning the planes.

After eight years of working tirelessly, Sigurd and others convinced President Harry S. Truman to sign an executive order in 1949 banning the planes. With the planes gone, remote resorts that were accessible only by airplane were closed.

Sig had become dean of Ely Junior College in 1936. He was a popular dean, and it was a stable, prestigious job, but he grew frustrated with its duties, and he longed to be outdoors or writing. In 1945, he traveled to England to work as a civilian in the US Army teaching zoology and geology to servicemen. After he returned in 1946, he spent only one more year as dean and then resigned to devote his life "to conservation, especially wilderness and writing of a type that will make people understand and be aware of what is at stake." He served as a wilderness ecologist with the Izaak Walton League and as a consultant to the president's Quetico-Superior Committee, an advisory group working to preserve the canoe country wilderness. Later he was named president of the National Parks Association and vice president (later president) of The Wilderness Society.

Sig enjoyed teaching US servicemen and traveling throughout Europe after World War II, while he worked as a civilian employee for the army.

These roles and others kept Sigurd front and center in the national wilderness scene and connected him with other visionaries and leaders in the movement, including Bob Marshall, who founded The Wilderness Society; Olaus Murie, director of the Izaak Walton League; and US Supreme Court justice

William O. Douglas. In 1954, he joined Douglas, Murie, *Washington Post* journalists, and thirty-some others on an eight-day hike, covering 189 miles, along the Chesapeake and Ohio Canal from Cumberland, Maryland, to Washington, DC, to publicize their opposition of a plan to develop the wild and primitive canal area. After working together on this cause, the group remained friends and stayed in close contact, joining forces on a number of conservation causes, but also traveling and canoeing together for fun.

Richard Leonard, president of the Sierra Club; Olaus Murie, president of The Wilderness Society; and Sig, president of the National Parks Association, in 1953

President Lyndon Johnson signed the Wilderness Act of 1964 in September of that year. The

Wilderness Act, which created the National Wilderness Preservation System that included the Boundary Waters Canoe Area, has been called one of the nation's greatest conservation achievements. The Wilderness Act also defined wilderness, allowed for the wilderness designation of federal wildlands, and set up a system for managing and protecting these lands. Sigurd played an essential role in the legislation, testifying before Congress, writing letters, building support locally and nationally, and helping to write the Wilderness Act.

Sig was involved for almost sixty years in every significant battle to save the wilderness near Ely. His activism didn't stop at Minnesota's borders, though. Through his work with The Wilderness Society; the Izaak Walton League; the National Parks Association; the advisory board on National Parks, Historic Sites, Buildings and Monuments; and as a consultant on wilderness and national parks to US secretary of the interior Stewart Udall, Sig played a key role in preserving wilderness throughout the United States, including Point Reyes National Seashore in California, Cape Cod National Seashore, Alaska's Arctic Wildlife Refuge, the Florida Everglades, and Indiana Dunes. He also named and helped establish Voyageurs National Park in northern Minnesota.

During those years, he took many trips to Washington, DC, and throughout the United States to meet with elected officials and speak at hearings and before groups and organizations. He also wrote articles and essays to express his strong convictions and sway decision-makers. He asked, "Must we repeat over and over the ghastly mistakes of the past, desecrating the landscape, destroying its wildlife, poisoning its clear waters, and leaving scars that will take thousands of years to heal?"

Five

The Power of Words

While Sigurd was in high school, the Ashland Chamber of Commerce sponsored an essay contest about the chamber's values. Sig didn't care about the organization or about the point of the essay, but he enjoyed writing, so he sat down, wrote an article, and submitted it. On the day the chamber of commerce announced that Sig had won first prize and a five-dollar gold piece, he realized that he had a gift for writing — or, as he said, "the ability to express myself."

After he and Elizabeth moved to Ely, Sig realized that he could share his passion about the outdoors and its spiritual importance in everyone's life by writing about it.

Becoming a published writer isn't easy, though, and over the years, Sig received many rejections for his writings. Publishers told him, "This stuff won't sell," and said he should include more adventure in his writing. In response he said, "I have adventures of the spirit," but, like all writers, he edited and revised his material many times before it was ready for publication. The first magazine article he wrote was turned down sixteen times, and his first and best-selling book, *The Singing Wilderness*, was rejected by many publishers before one accepted it. It was published in 1956 and quickly surged onto the *New York Times* Best Sellers list. Sig was ecstatic and proud. He was fifty-seven years old.

TELEPHONE LONGACRE 5-5481   CABLE ADDRESS BOBHAR

ROBERT THOMAS HARDY, INC.

PLAY-BROKERS AND AUTHORS' AGENTS

JANE HARDY, PRESIDENT

55 WEST 42ND ST., NEW YORK CITY

LONDON REPRESENTATIVE, CURTIS' BROWN, LTD.

May 8th, 1939.

Dear Miss Olson,

You write charmingly, but you will never sell, until you learn to put your perfectly lovely writing around a real plot. For instance---take the trout story. It has all kinds of possibilities. The atmosphere and background are lovely. But let Grandmother, *story* tell the little boy a story---letting it, also, remain in the background, but tying it up somehow, with the present life of the child, or of whatever you will. The theme of The Pines is too slight, as well. Both of these lovely things are sketches, and not really stories at all. Remember, the reader wants complications and a climax. I believe that you can do it, but it will take work, and a different viewpoint. Don't feel that you have to "write down." Quite the contrary. In the trout story, the mother and father of the child might be the new motivation--a story connecting the three generations. Do you see?

Sincerely,

Sigurd Thorn Olson
Ely, Minn.

Of Sig's many rejection letters, this one was especially embarrassing, because the agent assumed he was a young woman.

Over the next twenty-five years, Sigurd wrote eight more books. His second, *Listening Point*, recounted stories of his cabin and personal retreat. *The Lonely Land* was an account of the voyageurs and his own voyageur expeditions. Minnesota's senator Hubert H. Humphrey wrote to Sig in 1962, "My young son, Douglas, age 13, has been reading your excellent book entitled 'The Lonely Land.' He has enjoyed it so much. He insists that his Dad take him up into the north country next summer. You better prepare for some visitors because I am confident we are going to be up your way for some fishing and good outdoor recreation. Just wanted you to know that we enjoyed your book. We are proud of you. As ever, your friend."

Runes of the North, Sig's fourth book, told of legends of the Native Americans and the North. His autobiography, *Open Horizons*, was published in 1969 and was his fifth book. *The Hidden Forest* combined the nature photography of Les Blacklock with Sigurd's nature writing. *Wilderness Days* included photographs and drawings and compiled selected essays from his previous books season by season. Next, *Reflections from the North Country* showcased Sigurd's wilderness philosophy based on his many speeches. Sigurd completed his last book, *Of Time and Place*, shortly before he died. It was published in 1982. In it he reminisced about his experiences in the wilderness.

Despite his successes, Sigurd struggled with depression and even contemplated suicide. He had many dark, unhappy, and painful times. Early in his career he wrote, "Yesterday was almost unbearable and today it is worse. I do not think I can continue another moment. Everything about my life here seems impossible." Sigurd's struggles were hard on his family. Over time, he conquered the hopelessness he felt by finding his passion and acting on it to accomplish something worthwhile. The realization that his ultimate purpose in life was to preserve the wilderness sustained and drove him to take on a national role in the wilderness preservation movement. Later he said that only when people "work for something bigger than themselves for an ideal that will benefit all mankind will they find real peace."

During his lifetime, Sigurd wrote hundreds of articles about the wilderness for magazines such as *Sports Afield, Field & Stream*, and *Boys' Life*. He also wrote a column for the *Minneapolis Star Journal* and later a column syndicated by the North American Sportsman's Bureau called "America Out of Doors." Sig had a remarkable ability to capture the wilderness experience and the effect nature has on people. When people read Sig's poetic writings, they felt as if they

Sigurd wrote a syndicated newspaper column called "America Out of Doors" that focused on outdoors issues.

knew the area intimately even if they had never been there. They were easily convinced that wilderness had to be protected and that they must do what they could to help. Sig received thousands of letters from fans who were touched by his writings. They told him over and over, "You wrote what I felt."

Sig and his fans shared a mutual love for nature, which created a strong bond. Many asked for advice and revealed intimate details of their lives. Some told him that they thought of him as a friend even though they had never met. Sigurd was a faithful correspondent. He acknowledged most of the letters he received and often established relationships with those who had written to him. He responded to more than one fan by writing, "I also feel as though I know you too, and should we have the pleasure of meeting, I am sure we would hit it off as though we had known each other a lifetime." For a time Sig wrote in the family's small home, which was challenging for him and for the family. In 1937 he moved the family garage into the yard and converted it into a writing retreat. In this writing retreat, or "shack," he could get away from the telephone, his family, visitors, and other distractions. The writing shack was a warm, inviting place. A red braided rug covered the floor. Sig could look out the windows and see wildlife or the wind blowing the trees in his yard. At first, he would spend hours after his job at the college every day writing at a manual typewriter on his heavy wood desk. Later, after he resigned, he wrote during most waking hours when he wasn't fighting for the wilderness in Washington, DC, or other places. One morning he wrote to a friend,

Dear Winthrop,

Back home again after many weeks of absence all over the country, the far west, the southwest, the Everglades of Florida, Washington, DC and places in between. It is five in the morning and I am out in my writing place away from the house. It is ten below and the pines and

balsams are heavy with snow. Through the trees I get glimpses of town and the glitter of Christmas tree lights. Not a sound, but the soft moaning of the wind. It is good to be back where I belong away from crowds and planes, noise and speed.

Sig wrote in a garage that he turned into a writing shack. For a while, Sigurd wished that his middle name was Thorne (Thorne was his wife's mother's last name), and he signed his articles Sigurd Thorne Olson or Sigurd T. Olson. When their first son was born, Elizabeth and Sig named the baby Sigurd Thorne Olson, and Sigurd went back to using Sigurd F. Olson. The F stood for Ferdinand.

The shack was filled with his papers in piles and in boxes stacked high, rolled up maps, books, rocks, other items he'd found in nature, and photos of him with friends. In the corner a pair of snowshoes leaned against the wall, ready for a walk in the snow. The writing shack stands there today just as Sig left it.

Six

Never Give Up

Sig Olson's guiding philosophy was, "A man fights for the land he loves, and if he loves it enough he will never give up." Sig never wavered from his beliefs, but he was practical, and he learned that in order to accomplish great things, sometimes you have to compromise. Before President Lyndon Johnson signed the Wilderness Act in 1964, creating the National Wilderness Preservation System, Sig had worked closely with US senator Hubert Humphrey from Minnesota to gain support for the landmark legislation. While the Wilderness Act was considered a major victory for conservationists, it did allow for practices like logging and motorized vehicle use in wilderness areas. Sig was unhappy with the compromise, but he and the other conservationists wanted the bill to pass and realized some concessions were necessary.

When a fellow conservationist and former student, Bill Rom, questioned him about logging that was taking place in the Superior Roadless Area, Sig defended the US Forest Service, because he believed that the timber was diseased and that clear-cutting the tract was the best way to prevent a forest fire.

He acknowledged that this solution wasn't appealing in the short term, but he felt it was the best option for the future of the forest. (Later, his thinking on the matter evolved, and he stood firm against any clear-cutting.)

Sig was well-known and loved throughout the United States, but life in a small town wasn't always easy. People in northeastern Minnesota were angry that he wanted to place restrictions on the wilderness. They thought that they would lose their jobs and their way of life if they weren't allowed to use the wild places as they had in the past. The townspeople felt that Sig had betrayed his community, and Sig and Elizabeth became two of the most unpopular residents of Ely. People crossed to the other side of the street to avoid them. Fellow parishioners moved away from them in church. Clerks refused to serve them at the grocery store. The mayor referred to him as a "far-fetched dreamer," and others swore at Sig and Elizabeth and called them obscene names.

Once Sig met a good friend and former student on the street. When he yelled, "Hello, Jack," he was greeted with only a grunt. Neighbors scowled. Letters to the editor were printed in the local papers making false accusations about Sig's work to preserve the environment. One accused him of being "a peddler of two-faced propaganda," and another charged that he was in the fight only because as a wilderness guide he would benefit financially. One of his critics stated in reference to Sig, "One can question his motives in trying to segregate a large part of the recreational section of the country for the exclusive use of his customers." To counter the attacks on his character, Sig sold his outfitting business in 1951.

It was a lonely time for Sig and Elizabeth. Most of the other conservationists involved in the environmental movement lived outside the area, allowing them to escape the hostility, but Sig and Elizabeth lived in Ely, at the heart of the battle. They could not flee the fury directed at them. Those times were a harsh test of standing up for what they believed, and once again, they never backed down. Sig never fought back with rude or aggressive behavior. He remained calm even during intense arguments, because he understood where his neighbors were coming from, even though he didn't agree with them. Sig told a fellow activist in a letter, "It is easy to carry on this sort of cold warfare when away from this town, but to live here and face it every minute is another matter. … I suppose anyone who espouses a cause as controversial as this must expect attack and defamation of character."

The worst example of the hostility came during a congressional hearing held in Ely in 1977 to consider a bill that would ban motors, logging, and mining in the Boundary Waters Canoe Area. That July morning, as Sig walked up to the school building where the hearing was being held, a stuffed dummy hung from one of the logging trucks parked in front. A lump swelled in Sig's throat, and he inhaled deeply. The dummy, a likeness — an effigy — of Sig, had been hung there to scare him and the

Just three years earlier, the town of Ely had honored Sig. Now they considered him a traitor. Area residents wanted the freedom to snowmobile, drive motorized boats, or sell the timber from the wilderness area. Because of his national stature, Sig received the brunt of their anger.

others who were fighting for the preservation of the wilderness.

More than a thousand people crammed into the school for the emotionally charged hearing. When Sigurd stood to testify, the unruly, intimidating crowd jeered and booed him. Without flinching, he waited patiently to speak until the hecklers quieted down. "My name is Sig Olson, my home Ely, Minnesota," he began. He reminded the audience that "if any of these battles to preserve the BWCA had been lost, there would be no wilderness to argue about today." He also urged that "the time for action and immediate passage is now. I have crisscrossed the BWCA and its adjoining Quetico Provincial Park by canoe countless times since my early guiding days. This is the most beautiful lake country on the continent. We can afford to cherish and protect it. Some places should be

Sigurd, left, at the BWCA hearing in Ely. Later he said, "I have been facing this same sort of opposition for the past fifty years."

preserved from development or exploitation for they satisfy a human need for solace, belonging, and perspective. In the end we turn to nature in a frenzied chaotic world, there to find silence — oneness — wholeness — spiritual release." He turned around and returned to his seat.

In 1978, the BWCA bill declaring the Boundary Waters Canoe Area a wilderness area passed and was signed into law by President Jimmy Carter. It was a huge victory for Sig and other conservationists.

Sig Olson spent his whole life fighting for the wilderness, and he never felt like the battle was over. In 1981, US Department of the Interior secretary James Watt, who was serving under President Ronald Reagan, wanted to award him its highest civilian honor, the Conservation Service Award. Sig refused to accept the award because of his unhappiness with the Reagan administration's track record on wilderness protection. He told a friend that Interior Secretary Watt was "doing his [best] to destroy the environment."

Seven

Listening Point

For many years, Sig yearned to have a cabin in the wilderness. In 1955, when he was in his mid-fifties, he bought twenty-six acres of land near the shoreline of Burntside Lake, not far from Ely. Ancient green stones left on this land by a glacier ten thousand years earlier reminded him of the human connection to all things in the natural world, present and past. After searching the area around Ely, he bought an old log building, disassembled it, and moved it to his land. Sig and Elizabeth put much thought into the placement of the cabin. At first they planned to place it near the shoreline, but they realized that doing so would mar the view of the lake and shoreline for others. They built a stone foundation back in the trees and rebuilt the

Sig found inspiration for his writing at Listening Point. He wrote some of the chapters for his book *Listening Point* there and had planned to write more at his cabin, but he never did.

one-room cabin there to keep the lake view as natural as possible. They gathered stones on the property to build a fireplace and later built a sauna nearby.

Sig and Elizabeth welcomed friends, family, and even Sig's publisher, Alfred Knopf, and other conservation leaders to visit Listening Point.

At the cabin, Sig and Elizabeth could escape all the stress of everyday life. One evening, they picked blueberries along the shore and then launched their canoe on the lake. As they paddled slowly along, Sig baited a hook and cast a line with his fishing pole. It wasn't long before he felt a tug and reeled up a small bass. The setting sun cast a glow on the lake, and they floated in the tranquility. As he wrote in a letter to one of his fans, "All the fury and turmoil of the world outside seems so far away and almost unreal, all that counts is the fact we are here."

Sig loved sitting with his grandchildren in the steamy sauna at Listening Point. There he told them stories about how fawns got their spots. In between the stories, Sig hummed. When he and the children couldn't stand the heat one moment more, they made a mad dash to the dock and then dove into the chilly water of Burntside Lake. Sig's laughter rolled out across the bay. For breakfast they made blueberry pancakes and bacon. Afterward, Sig waited for his chipmunk friends to arrive, lured by the tantalizing aroma, so he could share the meal with them.

Sig and Elizabeth's daughter-in-law Vonnie described the cabin as a "listening post" for the wilderness and suggested they name it Listening Point. They loved the idea. As Sig said, "Everyone has a Listening Point somewhere."

Sig especially loved the silence and the sounds of nature at Listening Point. In his mind, he also heard the voices of friends and loved ones who had visited him there. Sometimes they were loud, other times like "soft whispers in the breeze." While at Listening Point, he saw countless animals, including coyotes, rabbits, porcupines, mink, deer, and a diversity of birds. One late February morning, he arrived at Listening Point to discover the tracks of two bobcats. Thrilled by the opportunity to see these elusive cats, he abandoned his

Through the years, the existence of Listening Point became well-known. It wasn't always the quiet spot Sig had envisioned, but he loved spending time there anyway. After he died, his ashes were scattered at Listening Point.

plans for the day and began to follow their tracks. He spent the next eight hours hiking through underbrush and swamps, over ridges, and along the shore as he traced their trail. Midafternoon, he sat on a rock and scanned the landscape in hopes of catching a glimpse of them. As the sun went down, he returned to the woodpile where he had first seen signs of their presence and listened intently for their yowls. Instead, he heard the hoot of an owl. Yet, he didn't mind. Later he wrote that even the possibility of hearing bobcats "meant much to me, for like all the music of the wilds, this had meaning, too."

Listening Point is a popular destination for Sigurd's fans today. Inside the rustic one-room cabin, paddles decorate the walls, a canoe hangs

The Listening Point Foundation owns and cares for Listening Point. Listening Point was named to the National Register of Historic Places in 2007.

from the rafters, and a coffeepot waits on a burner. Visitors can tour the lakeshore property on Burntside Lake near Ely with a guide to experience the sounds, trees, and rocks and see the cabin and sauna that Sig and Elizabeth built.

Eight
Passing the Torch

Sig had a unique ability to connect with people of all ages. Even when he was consumed with the important work of preserving wilderness throughout North America, he always took the time to listen, ask lots of questions, and encourage others. And he never took himself too seriously. He made silly faces and loved joking. He was calm and gentle, and his passion was infectious.

Sig had a special way of relating to others. He "planted hope in the hearts of young people." Former Minnesota governor Elmer L. Andersen said, "Sig conveyed a religious fervor and a depth of conviction that no one else I know succeeded in generating. Others could win adherence. He produced disciples." Governor Andersen meant that Sig inspired and motivated others to devote themselves to the wilderness cause like no one else had.

One way Sig instilled the love of nature in others was by having fun in the wilderness. Once he guided some men from Chicago who complained constantly about the weather, the food, and even the land. Sig became frustrated, especially with one man who complained most. "How can they not love it here like I do?" he wondered.

One afternoon he told the group that he would stay behind to make supper and encouraged them to take the canoes out without him. The complainer asked if Sig would dry his jeans over the fire while they were gone. When the men left, Sig took the buttons off the pants, hid the pants in his packsack, and put a piece of material in the fire along with the buttons. Then Sig lay down next to the fire. When the men returned, Sig sat up and rubbed his eyes, pretending he had fallen asleep and had accidentally let the jeans burn. The man saw the burned material and the buttons in the fire and yelled, "My pants! They're all burned up!"

Sig sheepishly offered to make the man some pants out of a scratchy old poncho. The man had no option but to wear the uncomfortable make-shift trousers for the rest of the journey. When they reached the end of the trip, Sig said, "Wait a minute. I think I've got your pants in my packsack," and he took the jeans out and handed them over. He always laughed when he remembered the incident, recalling, "It was a sad farewell for him but his two pals laughed with me [that] day."

Sig knew that he wouldn't be around forever to keep fighting to save the wilderness, yet he realized that the threats would continue. He expected younger generations to keep up the fight to preserve wild places like the Boundary Waters Canoe Area. He reminded them, "There is a need for constant vigilance if the area is to be preserved." And in a reply to a young fan he wrote, "The continuance of the wilderness is in the hands of young [people]. … Long after I am gone there will be problems and new battles to win."

Later he wrote, "That is really our fight, to protect the wilderness canoe country for the youth of America and to keep it possible for them to enjoy a primitive experience. … Where else in America can young people have so much healthful fun as out on a canoe trip?" Sig believed the Boundary Waters Canoe Area to be especially meaningful for children. He explained, "After seeing [the Boundary Waters], youth goes home truly conservation-minded, with a vision of green forests and pure water to work for the betterment of their own community."

Sig shared his love of the wilderness with his grandchildren. He had a special relationship with his grandson Derek, in part because of a common love of nature.

One summer night, Sig slept under a pine tree in the wilderness with six-year-old Derek. They lay in sleeping bags near the flickering light of a campfire and gazed at the stars in the sky. Just as he had done years earlier with his sons, Sig wove playful tales of moose and bear and fish. Then he told Derek the story of the dream net. "Derek, above us is an ancient net. The night is full of dreams both good and bad. Can you see them?" Derek nodded and admitted, "I can feel them around me." Sig reassured him, "Only the good dreams can get through that net," and Derek closed his eyes and went to sleep. After the fire had grown dark and the stars shone bright, Sig woke Derek to point out the constellations, including Great Bear, Cassiopeia, and the Pleiades.

Sig forged special relationships with other children too. Once he presented the daughter of a colleague, nine-year-old Jeannine, with his lucky rabbit's foot that had accompanied him on all of his canoe trips. He gave her brother a figure of a knight, and told him that when he grew up he would need to be a knight in shining armor to help save the wilderness. Sig and Jeannine began a dedicated pen pal relationship that lasted until Sig's death. They wrote many letters back and forth, sharing news of their recent trips into the wilderness or canoeing expeditions, and also their ideas, philosophy, and passion for nature.

"Dear Jeannine," Sig wrote, "I was delighted to get your letter telling me of your many adventures on your canoe trip all over the Quetico, which I know you love more than any other place in the world." In another letter, he wrote, "Who knows? You might be a writer some day and a conservationist, too. ... Love to my future Voyageur."

Toward the end of Sigurd's life, he was plagued by poor health. He battled cancer and shook constantly due to stress. But he still approached life with a sense of wonder, and his love for the wilderness never waned. He continued to write and spend time outdoors every day.

One bitterly cold January morning, he worked for a while in his writing shack and later went snowshoeing with Elizabeth. Elizabeth turned back because of a problem with her snowshoes, and while she was gone, Sigurd suffered a heart attack. He died there in his snowshoes doing what he loved most, enjoying the outdoors.

The day of the funeral his family discovered that he had left a note in his typewriter in his writing shack. It said:

A New Adventure is coming up
and I'm sure it will be
a good one.

Visitors to Sigurd Olson's writing shack can see this note, just as he left it.

Afterword

Sigurd Olson has been credited by many for saving the Boundary Waters Canoe Area. Without his constant vigilance, it is unlikely we would still have the virgin, untouched wilderness we know now. Today the BWCA includes over one million acres of land and is the most heavily used wilderness area in the United States, with more than 200,000 visitors a year. The largest wilderness area east of the Rocky Mountains and north of the Everglades, the BWCA provides a sanctuary for all kinds of wildlife, including black bears, timber wolves, moose, bald eagles, and numerous other bird species. It is the nation's largest lakeland wilderness, where visitors travel primarily by canoe, unlike most wildernesses where hiking and horseback are the main means of travel.

The BWCA is adjacent to Quetico Provincial Park in Canada. Quetico includes almost 1.2 million acres. Together the Quetico and BWCA cover about

2.3 million acres, an area slightly larger than Yellowstone National Park.

Open to anyone, the BWCA offers complete isolation and a remote adventure where young or old can know the thrill of wilderness and the sacred heritage that has been preserved. Children who visit the BWCA canoe, swim, and explore. They experience physical challenges and learn to value silence and to leave no trace. They escape from the noise and busyness that often overwhelm their daily lives.

Threats to the BWCA continue, such as hardrock mining and the construction of cell phone towers. Sig was correct when he said that the fight to protect the wilderness will never end. Unfortunately, compromises that helped pass the Wilderness Act in 1964, such as allowing logging and motorized vehicle use, continue to cause conflict in the BWCA.

Near the end of his life, young people asked Sig what his hope for the world was. He replied, "The hope for the world is in youth. You are the new generation. I am the old generation. You've got to carry on the battle to preserve beautiful places. The battle goes on endlessly. You've got to keep the flame alive, no matter what the obstacles. The whole world depends on you."

Sig dedicated his life to the outdoors. Because the wilderness fed his own soul, he knew how important enjoying and preserving the wilderness was for all people, past, present, and future. He urged, "We must look to the future — not the next decade, [but] a future of fifty, one hundred years, or a thousand. The important thing is to save places with wilderness quality to which the people of the future can repair for their spiritual well-being."

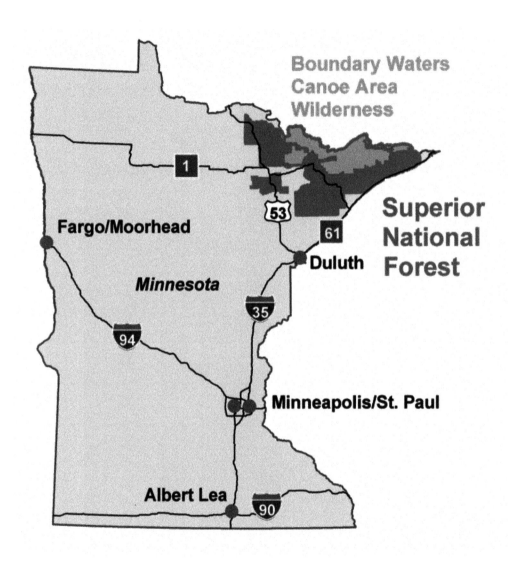

US Conservation Time Line

1872–First national park established — Yellowstone

1892–Sierra Club founded by John Muir

1899–Sigurd Ferdinand Olson born, Chicago, Illinois

1905–US Forest Service established

1909–President Roosevelt designates the wilderness area near Ely as the Superior National Forest

1921–Olson takes his first canoe trip in the wilderness area near Ely, Minnesota

1930–Shipstead-Newton-Nolan Act prohibits dams and logging within 400 feet of recreational waterways in Superior National Forest

1936–Olson named dean of Ely Junior College

1938–US Forest Service establishes Superior Roadless Area

1942–Olson begins writing a syndicated column, "America Out of Doors"

1949–President Truman signs an executive order banning airplane travel in the Superior Roadless Area

1953–Olson named president of National Parks Association

1956–Olson's first book, *The Singing Wilderness*, is published

1962–Olson becomes consultant on wilderness and national parks to Secretary of the Interior Stewart Udall

1963–Olson inducted into the Izaak Walton League Hall of Fame; National Wild and Scenic Rivers Act enacted

1964–Wilderness Act

1967–Olson receives the Sierra Club's highest award, the John Muir award

1968–Olson becomes president of The Wilderness Society

1970–First Earth Day; Clean Air Act; Creation of US Environmental Protection Agency (EPA)

1971–Voyageurs National Park established

1972–Northland College's Sigurd Olson Environmental Institute established

1973–Endangered Species Act

1978–Boundary Waters Canoe Area Wilderness Act

1981–Olson named first recipient of The Wilderness Society's highest award, the Robert Marshall Award

1982–Sigurd Olson dies snowshoeing near his home in Ely, Minnesota

1991–Olson inducted into the National Wildlife Federation Hall of Fame

2008–Intergovernmental Panel on Climate Change (IPCC) finds global warming trends largely caused by and can be reduced by human activities

Glossary

bluebill: a kind of diving duck with a bright blue bill; also known as greater scaup

concession: something done or agreed to in order to reach an agreement or improve a situation

conservationist: someone who works to promote or advocate for the conservation of natural resources

constellation: a cluster or group of stars that form a shape or pattern visible in the night sky

dam: a barrier that stops or contains water, often for the production of hydropower or electricity

depression: a medical illness when someone feels extremely sad or unhappy

effigy: a dummy, likeness, or figure representing a person

heckler: an individual who challenges a person or group, usually by shouting at a performance, event, or speech

humus: organic matter that comes from decaying plants and animals

kilowatt: a unit of energy

outfitter: a company or service that provides equipment and offers guiding services

portaging: carrying watercraft or supplies over land between two bodies of water

preservation: to preserve or protect something, often referring to natural resources

propaganda: information, true or not, used to influence an audience

ruff: hair growing around or on the neck of certain animals

spiritual: of sacred matters; concerning the mind, not bodily or material

virgin forest: an old-growth forest in its natural state before it has been changed or exploited by humans

voyageurs: French Canadian men employed by fur companies who traveled remote routes in canoes between Montreal and the Canadian Northwest to transport and trade goods and furs from 1650 to 1850

wilderness: an undeveloped area of land in its natural condition, uninhabited and undisturbed by human activity

Places to Visit

Minnesota

- **Boundary Waters Canoe Area (BWCA) or the Boundary Waters Canoe Area Wilderness (BWCAW).** Located in northeastern Minnesota, covering 150 miles along the Canadian border and bordered on the west by Voyageurs National Park. This is a true wilderness. There are eighty-eight entry points for boats. Motorboats are allowed in only some areas. Hiking, canoeing, and day and overnight permits are required.
- **Superior National Forest.** A boreal forest ecosystem west of Lake Superior. Contains the BWCA in its northern third.
- **Lake Superior.** The largest, coldest, and deepest of the Great Lakes and the world's largest freshwater lake. Borders Minnesota, Ontario, Wisconsin, and Michigan.
- **Ely.** Here you can visit Listening Point and Sig's writing shack. Contact the Listening Point Foundation to arrange a tour, http://listeningpointfoundation.org. Also see Vermilion Community College where Sig taught.
- **Voyageurs National Park.** Visitor centers include Rainy Lake, Kabetogama Lake, and Ash River. (www.nps.gov/voya/index.htm)

Canada

- **Quetico Provincial Park.** This protected wilderness is located north of the BWCA and west of Lake Superior in Ontario, Canada. A reservation and entry permit are required to travel here. (www.ontarioparks.com/english/quet.html)

Wisconsin

- **Ashland.** Visit the Northern Great Lakes Visitor Center and Northland College's Sigurd Olson Environmental Institute. (www.northland.edu/soei)
- **Sister Bay.** Sig spent his early years in this town in northern Door County along the shores of Green Bay.
- **Prentice.** Sig imagined he was Daniel Boone while he was growing up here.
- **Uhrenholdt Memorial Forest.** The land for this forest near Cable, Wisconsin, was donated by Elizabeth's family to the state of Wisconsin.

Other Places Sig Helped Protect

- **Arctic National Wildlife Refuge**, a national wildlife refuge in northeastern Alaska
- **Cape Cod National Seashore**, south and east of Boston, Massachusetts
- **The Florida Everglades**
- **Indiana Dunes National Lakeshore**, fifteen miles along the southern shore of Lake Michigan in Indiana, spanning from Gary to Michigan City
- **Point Reyes National Seashore**, thirty miles north of San Francisco, California

Take It Outside

Explore the outdoors by taking a nature walk. Identify plants and trees. Lie on the ground, like Sig did, and listen for the sounds of the Earth. What noises do you hear?

Think about the connection with history when outdoors. Imagine what the place looked like years ago. Who walked here before you? What did they think, wear, or experience? What storms have fallen here? What animals or creatures walked this same path?

Be active outside. Go camping with your family or attend a wilderness camp. Swim in a lake or canoe, kayak, or ride your bike. Go horseback riding or berry picking. In the winter, cross-country ski, ice skate, or snowshoe. Try dogsledding.

Develop a wildlife connection. Search for animal tracks and then research what you find. Even if you can't spend time in a true wilderness, there are usually many kinds of wildlife that live near us, even in urban areas. Look around for birds, deer, squirrels, geese, chipmunks, or rabbits. Do you see any nests? Go fishing or ice fishing. Try hunting.

Go outside on a clear night. Look up at the sky and identify constellations. Can you see the aurora borealis (known also as the northern lights)?

Learn the value of silence. Try to find a quiet spot outside. Don't talk or listen to music. Just sit or walk and allow yourself to think or not think. How do you feel?

Write about the wilderness. Grab a notebook and a pen or pencil. Go outside and find a comfortable spot to sit. What do you see? What do you hear? What do you smell? Try to write down in detail what your senses are experiencing. How does it make you feel? Describe your surroundings. What does the sun look like? Can you hear any birds singing or water rushing?

Develop a plan to contribute to protecting our natural resources. Undertake conservation practices, like recycling or conserving resources or energy. Research other possibilities. Are there issues you feel strongly about, like climate change or mining? If so, do your research and then write a letter to a policy-maker or to the local paper stating the problem, what you've learned, and what you believe.

Visit a state or national park. Stop by the ranger station or visitor center and learn about the park's history and unique features. What species of plants, trees, and animals exist here? What is the geology like? Walk one of the trails. Check out the forests, rivers, bogs, prairies, marshes, cliffs, or historic sites.

To Learn More

The Listening Point Foundation, http://listeningpointfounda-tion.org; PO Box 180, Ely MN 55731. Dedicated to furthering Sig's legacy of wilderness education and to preserving Listening Point. The foundation sponsors wilderness educational programs and publishes a newsletter and other materials. The foundation also sells Sig's books.

Website dedicated to Sigurd Olson:
www4.uwm.edu/letsci/research/sigurd_olson/contents.htm

Books by Sigurd Olson:
The Singing Wilderness
Listening Point
The Lonely Land
Runes of the North
Open Horizons
The Hidden Forest
Wilderness Days
Reflections from the North Country
Of Time and Place

Collections of Sig's essays, speeches, or writings:
Songs of the North: A Sigurd Olson Reader. Howard Frank Mosher, intro and ed.
Spirit of the North: The Quotable Sigurd F. Olson. David Backes, ed.
The Meaning of Wilderness: Essential Articles and Speeches. David Backes, ed.

*The Collected Works of Sigurd F. Olson: The Early Writings,
1921–1934.* Mike Link, ed.
*The Collected Works of Sigurd F. Olson: The College Years,
1935–1944.* Mike Link, ed.
The Wilderness World of Sigurd F. Olson, film. Ray Christensen and Steve Kahlenbeck.

Organizations:
Friends of the Boundary Waters Wilderness, www.friends-bwca.org. Focuses on protecting, preserving, and restoring the wilderness character of the BWCAW and the Quetico-Superior ecosystem. The organization provides information on such issues as sulfide mining, forest management, and tips for enjoying the wilderness while leaving no trace. Sponsors the Sigurd Olson Lecture Series, which brings visionary conservationists to speak in Minnesota on current natural resource issues. It also sponsors a program with YMCA Camp Menogyn and the Southeast Asian Youth Leadership Initiative to send economically disadvantaged young people on canoe trips in the BWCA.

Izaak Walton League, www.iwla.org/index.php?ht=d/Home/pid/175. Conserves, maintains, protects, and restores the soil, forest, water, and other natural resources of the United States and other lands.

National Parks Conservation Association, www.npca.org. Provides information on national parks and campaigns to protect them.

The Wilderness Society, http://wilderness.org. Provides information and other resources related to conservation and wilderness policy and campaigns. Join the WildAlert network to find out about important issues affecting the wilderness.

Will Steger Foundation, www.willstegerfoundation.org. Educates, inspires, and empowers people to engage in solutions to climate change.

Books for kids:

Kids Camp!: Activities for the Backyard or Wilderness (A Kid's Guide series) by Laurie Carlson and Judith Dammel; includes stories, projects, and activities.

True Green Kids: 100 Things You Can Do to Save the Planet, by Kim McKay and Jenny Bonnin.

Websites:

www.nps.gov/voya/forkids/index.htm. Information about Voyageurs National Park

www.ecologyfund.com/ecology/res_kid_home.html. Ecology website with games, activities, links, contests, and information on ecology issues

www.fs.fed.us/kids. Website for kids sponsored by the US Forest Service with information and activities related to nature and the outdoors

www.naturerocks.org. Website with information on playing in and exploring nature

Major Sources

Backes, David. Interview with Kristin Eggerling. July 2009.

Backes, David. *A Wilderness Within: The Life of Sigurd F. Olson.* Minneapolis: University of Minnesota Press, 1997.

Backes, David, editor. Anecdotes on website: www4.uwm.edu/letsci/research/sigurd_olson/contents.htm.

Christensen, Ray, and Steve Kahlenbeck. *The Wilderness World of Sigurd F. Olson,* film profile, Twin Cities Public TV, 1980, Listening Point Foundation.

Ely-Winton Historical Society. Archives and photo collection.

Kellogg, Jeannine. Interview with Kristin Eggerling. May 2010.

Listening Point Foundation. Photo archive.

Oetting, Robert B. "Sigurd Olson — Environmentalist." *Naturalist* Vol. 32. 1981:18. Print.

Olson, Robert K. Interview with Kristin Eggerling. October 2011.

Olson, Robert K. Personal photo collection.

Olson (Sigurd F.) Papers: Minnesota History Center, St. Paul, Minnesota. Essays, letters, journals, notes, and documents in Boxes 1, 2, 3, 4, 5, 6, 14, 15, 16, 17, 30, 31, 38, 41, 42, 59, 62, 64, 70, 73, 83.

Olson, Sigurd.. Recorded interview with John McKane, Robert Herbst and Newell Searle, May 27, 1976.

Olson, Sigurd F. Letters to Jeannine Kellogg, personal collection.

Olson, Sigurd F. *Listening Point.* New York: Alfred A. Knopf, 1958.

Olson, Sigurd F. *Open Horizons.* New York: Alfred A. Knopf, 1969.

Olson, Sigurd F. *Runes of the North*. New York: Alfred A. Knopf, 1963.

Olson, Sigurd F. *The Singing Wilderness*. New York: Alfred A. Knopf, 1956.

Olson, Sigurd F. "Wilderness Challenge." *Living Wilderness,* Summer 1970.

Proescholdt, Kevin. Interview with Kristin Eggerling. September 2009.

Proescholdt, Kevin, Rip Rapson, and Miron L. Heinselman. *Troubled Waters: The Fight for the Boundary Waters Canoe Area Wilderness*. St. Cloud, MN: North Star Press of St. Cloud, Inc., 1995.

Wick, Chuck. Interview with Kristin Eggerling. September 2009.

Index